Thanks for joining us
on the
Pelorus Mail Boat

Jan Killie Skipper 16th March '17

The
MARLBOROUGH
SOUNDS

Photographs by Graeme Matthews

Text by Heather Heberley

Thanks to Pelorus Mail Run, Beachcomber Cruises, John Bown, Allan and Shirley Wilson, and Nick Milne.

Published by Photo Image
Blenheim, New Zealand
Phone/Fax: +64 3 570 5655
Email: g.matthews@clear.net.nz
www.graememathews.co.nz

ISBN 978-0-9876554-3-1
Printed in Hong Kong 2012
Designed by Go Ahead Graphics, Christchurch
Photographs copyright © Graeme Matthews
Text copyright © Heather Heberley

The
MARLBOROUGH
SOUNDS

QUEEN
CHARLOTTE
SOUND
(TOTARANUI)

Cape Jackson

Titirangi
Bay

Port Gore

Waimatete
Bay

Anakakata
Bay

N
W E
S

Motuara Island

Furneaux Lodge

Ship Cove
(Meretoto)

Long Island

Onehunga
Bay

Onauku

Resolution
Bay

Anatohia
Bay

Punga Cove   Tawa Bay

Onauku
Bay

Endeavour
Inlet

QUEEN CHARLOTTE SOUND
(TOTARANUI)

East Bay

Pickersgill
Island

Dryden Bay

Blumine Island
(Oruawairua)

Otanerau
Bay

Bay of
Many Coves
(Miritu Bay)

ARAPAWA ISLAND

Ruakaka
Bay

Whekenui

Kumutoto
Bay

Blackwood
Bay

Double Bay

East Head

Torea Bay
(Torea Moua)

Dieffenbach Point

Ngaruru
Bay

TORY CHANNEL

Lochmara
Bay

Allports Is.

Onahau
Bay

Christys
Bay

Maraetai
Bay

Curious
Cove

Hitaua
Bay

Waikawa
Bay

Whatamango
Bay

Onapua
Bay

Anakiwa

GROVE ARM

Momorangi
Bay

Ngakuta
Bay

Picton
Harbour

Okiwa Bay

The Grove

Waikawa

Havelock

QUEEN CHARLOTTE DRIVE

Picton

QUEEN CHARLOTTE SOUND

Queen Charlotte Sound is the easternmost of the Marlborough Sounds. All these sounds are drowned river valleys which were created by immense tectonic forces that heaved, twisted, pushed up, lowered and shattered the rock.

When Captain Cook first visited the area in 1769 he found Maori settlements throughout the sounds. Stories handed down through Maori whakapapa tell how Kupe, the Hawaiki chief and navigator, discovered New Zealand in the 10th century while chasing a giant octopus known as Te Wheke o Muturangi across the Pacific. He eventually killed it at the entrance to Tory Channel.

The area was the base for whaling throughout the 19th and early 20th century until the Perano whaling station closed in 1964 and it was this trade which brought the first white settlers to the area in 1829 and where New Zealand's first white child was born in 1831.

Antimony was discovered in the hills at the head of Endeavour Inlet in 1874 and until it closed in 1892 there were over 100 miners working in the horizontal mine shafts. A significant amount of gold was taken directly from quartz reefs at Cape Jackson.

Many guest houses and lodges operate throughout the sounds giving visitors a wide choice of accommodation with Punga Cove, Furneaux Lodge and Bay of Many Coves Resort being the better known in Queen Charlotte Sound. In other bays holiday homes built so close together, create an almost suburban look, while others are tucked into secluded coves almost hidden from sight by the regenerating bush.

As larger blocks of land were cleared cattle and sheep were farmed. Farmers sent their cream out on the weekly mail boat which was in those days known as the Cream Run. Today only one or two farms of any size remain and land that hasn't been

swallowed up by pine trees has reverted to native bush. Marine farms are growing with salmon and mussels thriving in the pristine water, one of the most important factors in successful marine farming.

Picton, the gateway of the South Island, is the northern terminus of the South Island's road and railway networks. Kaipupu Point divides the head of Picton Harbour into two bays. The interisland ferries and cruise ships berth on the eastern side of the point and Shakespeare Bay on the western side is Picton's deep water logging port.

The hub of Picton is the busy waterfront where tourists can choose between one of the many water taxis, charter boats, or the renowned mail boat to take them to the northern entrance of the sound as far as Cape Jackson where the Russian cruise ship Mikhail Lermontov hit rocks before sinking in Port Gore in 1986. Or they can follow the interisland route through Tory Channel to its entrance, the place where Kupe is said to have discovered New Zealand.

The *Kaitaki* looms out of the mist in Picton Harbour.

Picton's waterfront; the hub of Picton.

From the air all Picton's streets lead to the sea.

A panoramic view of Picton Harbour from the lookout on the Queen Charlotte Drive.

Yachts from the Queen Charlotte Yacht Club head out for an afternoon's racing on Picton Harbour.

Logs stacked up waiting for shipment at Shakespeare Bay.

Above: Waikawa Bay and its many moored boats and large marina.
Opposite: Looking down Picton Harbour towards Mabel Island.

A quiet spot for a bach in Blackwood Bay.

Yacht moored in Ruakaka Bay.

Above: Luxury accommodation at Bay of Many Coves Resort.

Opposite: Aerial view looking across Bay of Many Coves to the Outer Sounds and Northern Entrance.

Shafts of sunlight break through the clouds around the top of Mt. Stokes, the highest point in the Sounds.

The rugged western tip of Long Island.

Above: Blumine Island on a placid winter's day.
Opposite: *"As idle as a painted ship upon a painted ocean"*; from 'the Rime of the Ancient Mariner', S.Coleridge.

Above: The western end of Long Island with Cape Koamaru on the right as cumulus clouds build over the North Island.
Opposite: Aerial view looking westwards up Queen Charlotte Sound in the early morning light.

Evening in Endeavour Inlet; from Punga Cove.

Punga Tree ferns, Endeavour Inlet.

Mailboat cruise at Ship Cove.

Ship Cove and the monument to Captain Cook.

Above: Department of Conservation worker Leanne, after cutting the lawn at Ship Cove.
Opposite: Ship Cove still retains the native bush which once covered all the Sounds.

Passengers off the mailboat have a closer look at the monument.

A Maori carving guards the bridge at Ship Cove; a bridge over the same stream that Captain Cook obtained fresh water from for his ship and crew.

Motuara Island, as seen from Ship Cove.

At Ship Cove this carved pou whenua tells the legend of Kupe and Te Wheke o Muturangi.

Water reflections take on the look of molten metal.

Boat wake leaving Ship Cove.

Above: The sun sets behind Mt. Stokes, Endeavour Inlet.

Opposite: The Queen Charlotte Track is renowned for its native bush, bird-life and spectacular views.

Delivering supplies to a waiting boat at Cape Jackson.

Dusky dolphins and Shearwater birds feeding together.

A calm morning in Hitaua Bay.

A shaft of late afternoon sunlight strikes a hillside in Endeavour Inlet.

Above: A resident in Eerie Bay has company to collect her mail.
Opposite: Afternoon cloud surrounds the head of Endeavour Inlet.

Early morning, Hitaua Bay, Tory Channel.

Tory Channel Entrance, looking out to Cook Strait.

Above: '*Arahura*' (pathway to the dawn) travels through Queen Charlotte Sound.
Opposite: Hostile cliffs guard the narrow entrance to Tory Channel.

Dusky Dolphins (*Lagenorhynchus obscurus*) frolic.

Headland between Resolution Bay and Endeavour Inlet.

Above: Fiery evening sky, Resolution Bay.
Opposite: A red-billed gull (*Chroicocephalus scopulinus*) shows perfect symmetry in flight.

Heading into Endeavour Inlet.

Evening clouds, looking east to Long Island and the Northern Entrance.

Cirrus clouds over Endeavour Inlet.

One of the many cruise ships that visit Picton each summer.

Above: Looking west down the Grove Arm of Queen Charlotte Sound at twilight.
Opposite: Queen Charlotte Sound, as seen from the Queen Charlotte Drive.

A yacht finds a beautiful anchorage in Governor's Bay, as seen from the Queen Charlotte Drive.

Ngakuta Bay, Queen Charlotte Sound.

Momorangi Bay, a popular camping spot in summer.

Fishy letterbox, The Grove.

Above: Letterboxes, The Grove.
Opposite: Boats swing gently on their moorings in the still waters at The Grove.

Shags gather together in the fog; Tirimoana, at the head of Queen Charlotte Sound.

Adventure company storage shed near Anakiwa with some bright artwork by local artist Sirpa Alalääkkölä.

Driftwood piled up in the Mahakipawa Arm.

Looking eastwards up the Mahakipawa Arm.

PELORUS SOUND

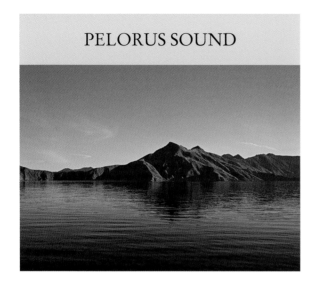

PELORUS SOUND

Pelorus Sound, the largest of the Marlborough Sounds was named by Lieutenant Chetwode, who in 1838, carried out the first survey of the sound in HMS *Pelorus*. It winds south from the north western waters of Cook Strait for about 55 kilometres until it reaches the small town of Havelock which lies between Blenheim and Nelson. It is here that one of New Zealand's most strategically placed mussel processing factories operates and why Havelock capitalises on its name as the Greenshell Mussel Capital of the World.

The first commercial harvest of the green-lipped mussels in the Marlborough Sounds was on 11 September 1971. But it was to be another six years before any large commercial crops were harvested and since then mussel farming has continued to increase with the main concentration in the Pelorus and Keneperu Sounds.

Long before mussels brought wealth into Havelock, sawmills sprung up throughout the area. From 1865 extensive tracts of land were cleared of native bush. Mills were set up on flat land to mill the trees close to where they were logged. Down at the jetty the timber was stacked into bundles and hauled onto the deck of a waiting ship using man power and pulleys. Once on deck the timber was stacked for the sea voyage. The sounds waterways were ideal for the transportation of timber without the need of expensive ports or land travel, to supply New Zealand's growing demand for native timber. The last timber mill closed in 1939.

Maud Island in the outer Pelorus was stripped of its giant trees to make way for farming and was grazed intensively for many years. Today the 310-hectare island is an important nature reserve with entry by permit only or permission from the Department of Conservation. Its predator-free status makes it a haven for many native and rare species.

Deep in the Pelorus on the eastern shores of Crail Bay is Hopai. Every year, in early January, more than 1000 people arrive at Hopai for the annual Sports Day, held on land farmed by the Gerard family. Records of this event date back to 1920.

As in Queen Charlotte, isolated residents and holiday makers rely on the mail boat for their mail and grocery deliveries. Many people have lived in their homes for years and tell people they'll have to be carried out in a box. Others row out in a dinghy to meet the boat to collect mail and stores. Some wade into the water to collect their goods off the mail boat's bow. But there are many who never forget the stories their grandparents told them before there was a mail boat. Stories of them catching the flood tide to row into Havelock to do the shopping, then pack everything into the dinghy and row home with the ebb tide.

The history and grandeur of these sounds is unique, but it is these people, many of whom still walk in the footsteps of their ancestors, who make these sounds memorable.

Aerial view of Havelock, at the head of Pelorus Sound.

Above: Havelock marina on a still morning.
Opposite: Red-billed gulls gather in flocks on the mud flat.

The main street, State Highway 6, passes through Havelock.

Havelock township as seen from the Queen Charlotte Drive.

Oystercatchers (*Haematopus unicolor*) congregate to feed at low tide.

Havelock marina.

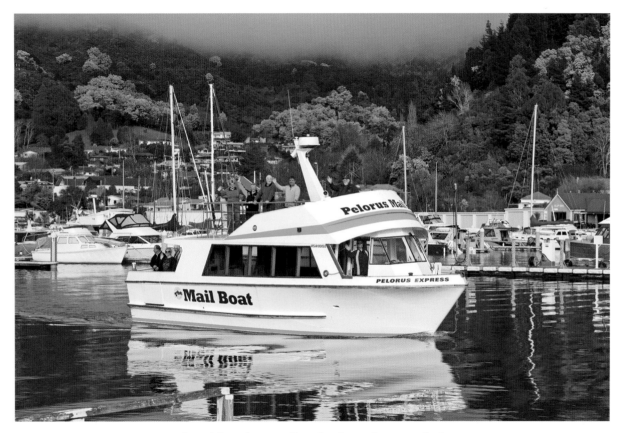

Above: The Pelorus mailboat heads out from Havelock.
Opposite: Aerial viewpoint above Cullen's Point looking down Pelorus Sound.

Johnson's barge taking pine-logs to Havelock. Cleared hillsides can be seen in the background.

Clearing fog on a still morning, Nydia Bay.

Above: Residents of Nydia Bay wait for the mail.
Opposite: Nydia Bay.

Hector's Dolphin (*Cephalorhynchus hectori*) found only in New Zealand, is one of the smallest dolphins.

Native bush grows down to the water's edge in Nydia Bay.

Narrow passages, islands, clouds and sea stretch into infinity.

An old boatshed shows the ravages of time; Pokokini, South East Bay.

The expansive view from Te Rawa.

A gannet (*Morus serrator*) skims the water. They can dive vertically from 30 metres, reaching speeds up to 100 kilometres per hour.

Above: Delivering the mail to Bob and his dog at Yncyca Bay.
Opposite: A serene view of Pelorus Sound, looking towards Tawero Point.

A solitary boat heads towards the rising sun as it steams up the Apuau Channel, past Maud Island, Pelorus Sound.

A pod of Bottlenose Dolphins, Crail Bay.

The boat's wake disappears into the distance.

Mussel harvesting from a specially built craft.

Greenshell mussel (*Perna canalicula*) farm in South East Bay.

Bottlenose Dolphin (*Tursiops truncatus*) is one of the largest of the dolphin species.

Delivering the mail to Crail Bay involves some tricky maneuvering.

Greenshell mussel farm in Port Ligar.

Mist creeps over the ridge like a blanket, Clova Bay.

A Kunekune pig demands some food from the mailboat, Kaitata Bay.

Above: Calm water in Beatrix Bay.
Opposite: Delivering the mail to Pohuenui.

Sunlight lights up a headland in Beatrix Bay.

Bottlenose Dolphin (*Tursiops truncatus*), Crail Bay.

Above: Handing over the mail at Port Ligar.
Opposite: A symphony of sea and cloud, Pelorus Sound.

Above: Calm waters in the outer Sounds, looking towards the Chetwode Islands.
Opposite: The rugged hills of D'Urville Island. It is the eighth largest island in New Zealand.

Heading back to Tawero Point.

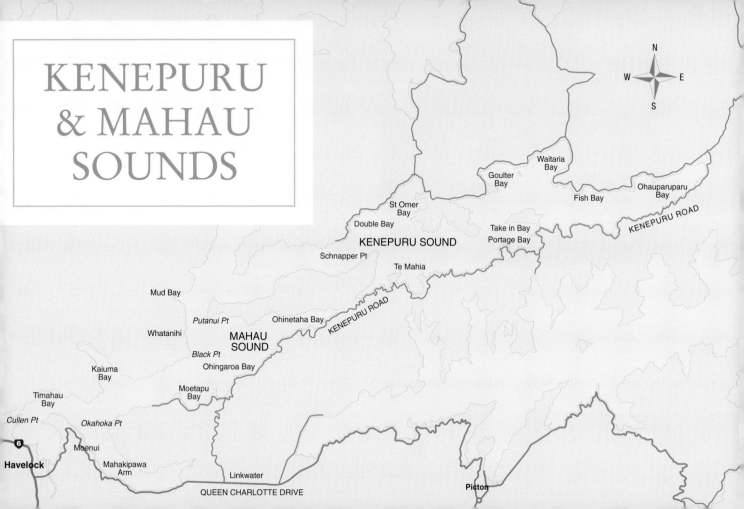

KENEPURU & MAHAU SOUNDS

N
W E
S

Waitaria Bay

Goulter Bay

Ohauparuparu Bay

Fish Bay

St Omer Bay

Double Bay

KENEPURU SOUND

KENEPURU ROAD

Take in Bay
Portage Bay

Schnapper Pt

Te Mahia

Mud Bay

Putanui Pt

Ohinetaha Bay

KENEPURU ROAD

Whatanihi

MAHAU SOUND

Black Pt

Kaiuma Bay

Ohingaroa Bay

Moetapu Bay

Timahau Bay

Cullen Pt

Okahoka Pt

6

Moenui

Mahakipawa Arm

Havelock

Linkwater

Picton

QUEEN CHARLOTTE DRIVE

KENEPURU & MAHAU SOUNDS

The Kenepuru is the third largest of the four sounds that make up the Marlborough Sounds and Mahau the smallest. Early settlers named the Kenepuru Coniston Water, after the third largest lake in the English Lake District. This sound is separated from Queen Charlotte by a narrow arm of land and it is along this ridge-line the 71-kilometre Queen Charlotte Track runs from Ship Cove to Anakiwa.

Mt Stokes rises up from Kenepuru Head. It was named after Captain Stokes on HMS *Acheron*. At 1203 metres it is the highest point in the sounds and often shrouded in clouds giving it an air of mystery. Although no evidence has ever been found it was thought that John Moncrieff and Geoff Hood's plane might have crashed into the rugged bush-clad slopes during their attempt to be the first to fly between Australia and New Zealand in January 1928.

Farming is carried out at Kenepuru Head, Manaroa and Waitaria Bay where Waitaria School still operates. Built by families of early settlers in 1897 many of the pioneers' names can still be found on the current school roll.

As in the other sounds, trees were logged heavily within the Kenepuru and Mahau, but it is in the Kenepuru at the Skiddaw Reserve one can see what is claimed to be the only unlogged bush in the sound and drops right to the water's edge. The canopy of native trees with tree ferns pushing their fronds toward the sun filter the light to create a natural habitat for flowering plants that grow amongst the mosses and fungi below.

Many lodges, camp-sites and guest houses can be found in the Kenepuru. Te Mahia, Raetihi and Portage all come with a history. The Portage Hotel opened in 1912 and for many years was one of the most glamorous hotels in the sounds. It lies on the Kenepuru side of the narrowest piece of land which separates it from Queen Charlotte.

The name comes from the word 'portage' – to

carry boats and supplies overland and between water. When Captain James Cook visited the sounds in the 1770s he listed the Torea Saddle as being 'a place of portage.' Another settler, Robert Blaymires, who regularly carried his boat from Torea to Kenepuru during the mid-1800s gave the name Portage to the route.

At the head of Mahau Sound set in native bush and a deserted coastline stands Sherrington Grange owned by the Harper family. It is a working farmhouse where the family produce manuka honey and bouquet cheeses which are sold throughout New Zealand. The house is also run as a guesthouse.

For photographers and artists alike, the Marlborough Sounds are a treasure trove where scenes of such natural beauty can be captured forever, while others can watch and see a natural collage forming as islands, inlets and points seem to stack up one behind the other, while the ever changing colours of the bush, sea and sky merge into one glorious work of art.

Above: Looking back to Mahau Sound.
Opposite: Ancient Tree-ferns, Mahau Sound.

Looking towards the entrance to Kenepuru Sound.

Kenepuru Sound.

The sheltered bays and sandy beaches of Te Mahia, Kenepuru Sound.

Te Mahia, as seen from the Kenepuru road.

Above: Mussel farms create their own patterns in the calm waters of Kenepuru Sound.
Opposite: Kenepuru Sound under a striking sky.

Portage Hotel was named after the word portage; to carry boats between two waters.

Portage Hotel, Kenepuru Sound.

Above: Wharf at Portage.
Opposite: The head of Kenepuru Sound, with its turquoise-coloured waters.

Terns take flight at the water's edge.